Published by
Yale School of Architecture
P.O. Box 208242
New Haven, Connecticut 06511
www.architecture.yale.edu

ISBN: 978-1-63840-018-9
Library of Congress Control Number: 2022932483

This book is part of the Studio Book Series
published through the Dean's office.

Dean
Deborah Berke

Publications Director
Nina Rappaport

Editor
Ruike Liu

Copy Editor
Ann Holcomb

A Center for Victims of Domestic Violence in New Haven

Turner Brooks and Jonathan Toews
Advanced Design Studio
Yale School of Architecture

Alexander Velaise, 2020 Spring

Daoru Wang, 2020 Spring

Table of Contents

A Letter

from Hope Family Justice Center (HFJC) of New Haven

Hope Family Justice Center (HFJC) is part of a movement spreading across the world seeking how to best respond to victims of abuse. It is collaborating with existing providers to access direct and immediate services and care. It is a "one-stop-shop" that provides free and confidential "wraparound" services and care in a trauma-responsive environment that is Client-Centered, Strength-Based, and HOPE-Driven. A Family Justice Center (FJC) takes the best services that already exist in a given community and brings them all together under one roof. It is the co-location of a multidisciplinary team of professionals who work together to provide coordinated services to victims of family violence. It is a victim-centered, survivor-driven philosophy. The victim makes one trip to receive more efficiently delivered services.

The core concept of a Family Justice Center is to provide a single address where victims can go to talk to an advocate, plan for their safety, interview with a police officer, meet with a prosecutor, receive medical assistance, receive information on shelter, and get help with transportation. To receive basic needs, a victim seeks various services, sometimes from over 10 different agencies. In our current system, a victim would have to travel to each agency to receive services. In a typical domestic violence situation, a victim might need to seek services for herself and her children at New Haven criminal court, The Umbrella Center for Domestic Violence Services, Department of Children and Families (DCF), Yale Child Study Center, Legal Aid, and civil court.

Throughout police officers' career, they will respond to more domestic violence crimes than any other type of case. Domestic violence incidents are by far the most volatile situations that police officers will encounter. Domestic disputes accounted for 22% of line of duty deaths for officers from 2010 - 2014. If you look into the backgrounds of those that commit violent crimes, including gun violence, murders, mass shootings, and cop killings, you will find that most were committed by men who have a history of domestic violence. The shootings at the Fort Lauderdale airport; Virginia Tech, Orlando's Pulse nightclub, Las Vegas, and Parkland Florida—all were committed by men who had histories of abusing women. In the U.S., domestic violence costs $8.3 billion in expenses annually due to higher medical costs and lost job productivity by victims. Victims of intimate partner violence across the U.S. report an average of 7.2 days of work-related lost productivity per year. One of the significant outcomes to having a FJC in the community is the significant decrease in domestic homicides. In the 15 years after opening, the San Diego Family Justice Center saw a 95% reduction in domestic violence homicides. New Haven averages one domestic violence homicide a year.

Our plan is to have the Hope Family Justice Center (HFJC) located in downtown New Haven. We have identified a space that is within walking distance to the courthouses at 121 Elm Street and 235 Church Street, New Haven Legal Aid, and City Hall. It will be close to public transportation, including the bus connections at the New Haven Green, and rail connections at State Street and Union Station. Being close to public transportation is a high priority, considering that in the City of New Haven, more than one out of every four households and families are "zero-car"

households, with no car available. Being within walking distance to the Courthouse will allow prosecutors and victims to have a trauma-informed, safe, and confidential space in which to meet. This will result in reduced recantation and minimization by victims. We believe that the benefits of having access to public transportation, courthouses, and the ability for victims to meet with prosecutors in a trauma-informed space, far outweighs the cost. We are passionate about bringing the Hope Family Justice Center of Greater New Haven to our community. We need your support. Please visit our website at http://www.bhcare.org/page/32663 or contact us at 203-800-7204 for more information and to learn how to support this important cause, not only for the victims we serve, but also for our community.

In peace and hope,
Julie Johnson, HFJC Coordinator
Paola Serrecchia, HFJC Site Manager

Introduction
to the Studio Project

Family Justice Center and Domestic Violence

The concept of the "Family Justice Center" is a relatively new institution founded to deal with the issue of domestic violence. The institution has developed in the United States over the last few decades, partly based on a pioneering precursor founded in San Diego in 2002. There are now many similar concepts across America and throughout the world. The urgency of the family justice crisis has inspired New Haven's city government to integrate a Family Justice Center as a recognizable and accessible destination not far from the County Courthouse and the City Hall. A temporary facility for this organization, called the Hope Family Justice Center(HFJC), opened on Temple Street in late August 2019.

Turner Brooks was introduced to the concept of a family justice center through a fellow hockey parent, Julie Johnson, who he sat next to during a practice. A former police captain, Julie's current mission has been to initiate a family justice center in New Haven. She gave a graphic outline of the necessity for such a public institution devoted to this cause. She described a typical victim of family violence seeking help, and the difficulties. Not only was it hard to know who to contact for help, or where to go, but often victims needed to seek support from multiple experts, ranging from lawyers to detectives to therapists to psychologists to medical doctors, and/or other types of professionals. In a state of confusion as to where to go for help, having to make multiple trips to different destinations, absenting themselves from their jobs, and often having to provide care for young children, many victims simply give up on their search for assistance. Julie made it clear that one central hub housing all resources was urgently needed to set up "one-stop shopping."

Field Study

As an introduction to the project, students toured the new temporary facility in New Haven, met with the HFJC director Paola Serrecchia, chief city planner Aicha Woods, and other agency representatives, including local experts in the fields of social work, child psychology, emotional and physical trauma and recovery, law, and survivors of domestic violence. Yale psychiatrist Stan Walther spoke of how the brain can react to different spatial conditions. Similar dialogue with professionals was maintained throughout the semester with the development of the student projects.

The students interviewed the directors of Brooklyn Family Justice Center (BFJC), visited the Netherlands during travel week to meet with representatives of Blijf Groep (Stay Group) and Veiling Thuis (Safe Home), operators of domestic violence support centers, and toured a recently completed facility in Almere, just outside of Amsterdam. In the Netherlands, the students looked at other buildings deemed relevant to the project which invoked issues of "body and space"—especially the work of Aldo Van Eyck, including his Mother's House, the Orphanage, the Pastor Van Ars Church, Herman Herzberger's housing, as well as the human-scale organicism of the early-twentieth-century Amsterdam School. These projects had a deep influence on the student work as it was to evolve.

Fig. 1, Edward Hopper, *Rooms by the Sea*

Fig. 2, Joseph Mallord William Turner, *Landscape with a River and a Bay in the Background*

Fig.3, Yonah Freemark

Body and Space—Liminal Zone

In many ways, the design emphasis of the studio developed as the choreography between "body and space," proceeding from the public street into and through the various elements of the program inside the building in the search to find appropriate assistance. Liminal space, both in a physical and psychological sense, played a key role in the design of the Family Justice Center project, and the liminal zone itself became the subject of a preliminary design exercise at the beginning of the semester. Arriving at the Family Justice Center, the victim, already likely suffering trauma, must face the anxiety of transitioning from the exterior public realm of an urban space (street, courtyard, or alley, depending on which of the three given sites was selected by each student) to the interior of the relatively private and (for first-time visitors) unknown realm of the institution. The first assignment was to design an empathetic liminal zone that transitioned in a comfortable way between an exterior area of approach to the building and the interior that is first confronted—from where the victim is steered on to the appropriate counselor in another space somewhere further inside. In many ways, this concept of the liminal, or transitional space, became a primary guiding inspiration in the design process, in general. The concept choreographed appropriate spatial connections between different aspects of the program throughout the project.

Readings were assigned that were relevant to the liminal zone and the issue of the human body relating to space. Kent Bloomer and Charles Moore's *Body Memory and Architecture* clearly explains the relationship of the body to space through the investigation of the "haptic" sense. Franz Kafka's *The Burrow* describes a paranoid protagonist searching in his endless excavations for a passage from the exterior world to the safe haven of an interior realm burrowed into the earth. Gaston Bachelard's *Poetics of Space* was relevant in its discussion of the contrast, but also the direct, balanced connection and relationship between the "infinite" and the "intimate," as well as the transition between the two. Edward Hopper's *Rooms by the Sea (ca. 1882-1967)* [fig. 1] was invoked as an illustration of the inseparability of the infinite and finite condition: the ocean seen through the door representing the infinite, and, on the other side, the partial view of interior domesticity representing the finite. The luminous light on the blank wall in the center of the composition performs the role of the liminal "mediator," as it connects those two other conditions. In a very different way (reminiscent of the message in *Body, Memory, and Architecture*), the painting *Landscape with a Bay and a River in the Background* (ca.1835–1840), by William Turner, [fig. 2] presents an atmosphere that is so physically palpable that it surrounds and engages the body, comfortably transporting it into a tactile dimension.

A model [fig. 3] made by Yonah Freemark for a project called "liminal zone" clearly demonstrates, in an abstract manner, the gentle tactile navigation through such a transitional space. The density and configuration of the soft hanging balls can be adjusted by hand-operated pulleys for different conditions of passage.

Shuchen Dong, Spring 2020

Robin Hengyuan Yang, Spring 2020

Design Brief

The program of the 20,000-square-foot facility included a public lobby, semi-private check-in, child day care, counseling, medical exam rooms, legal offices, criminal investigators' offices, group therapy rooms, job training and lecture rooms, staff offices, as well as family lounges, kitchens, and exercise rooms.

Other related facilities were investigated and became additional elements in the program. This included sleeping areas or studio apartments for victims who cannot safely return home, long-term childcare, an exterior courtyard or recreation space, a cafe, an area for job training and rehabilitation programs, and additional space for autonomous groups, such as legal aid/legal rights organizations.

Initial Prompts

Civic vs. Discrete : How does the building balance the visible presence of the institution with the anonymity and discretion required for incoming clients?

The Internal Street: How do multiple autonomous agencies coexist around a semi-public interior space? What are the specific requirements for interaction and exchange with a doctor, lawyer, counselor, and police officer?

Effect of Trauma: How do the psychological effects of trauma affect perception in an institutional building? What is the direct experience of space and material relative to notions of "comfort," "warmth," and "community"? How can you articulate a therapeutic environment?

Children's Perspective: How do children perceive space, material, light, and texture? How are they separated from and then reconnected to parents and other adults? What are the experiential differences?

Multi-Agency
Family Justice Center Structure

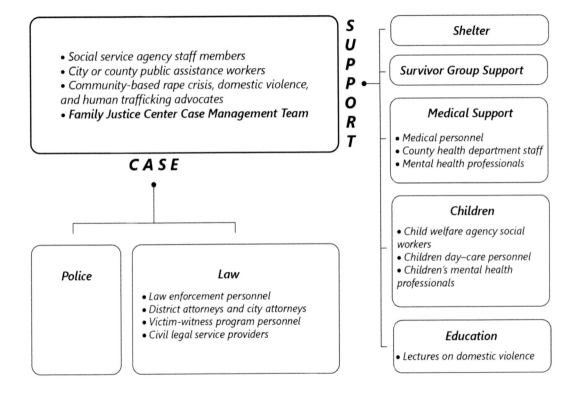

- Social service agency staff members
- City or county public assistance workers
- Community-based rape crisis, domestic violence, and human trafficking advocates
- *Family Justice Center Case Management Team*

CASE

Police

Law
- Law enforcement personnel
- District attorneys and city attorneys
- Victim-witness program personnel
- Civil legal service providers

SUPPORT

Shelter

Survivor Group Support

Medical Support
- Medical personnel
- County health department staff
- Mental health professionals

Children
- Child welfare agency social workers
- Children day–care personnel
- Children's mental health professionals

Education
- Lectures on domestic violence

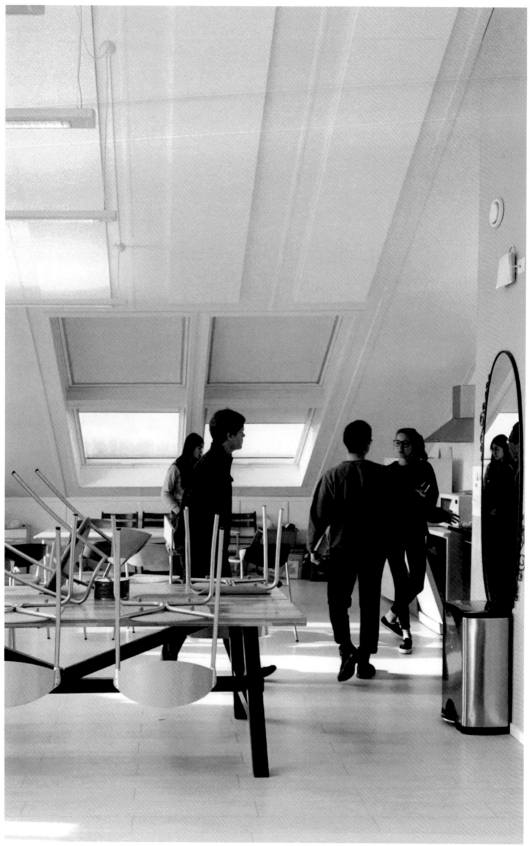

Common space–The Orange House (established by Blijf Groep), Almere, Netherlands

Space Precedents
Orange House in Almere, the Netherlands

When the victim of domestic violence and the perpetrator do not want to stay in the same room, or it is dangerous for the interviewees to stay together, they will be separated into two adjacent rooms where there is a staff-only door at the back.

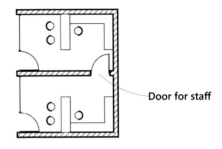

Door for staff

A chair with a tall back and two partitions on both sides creates a private space to make people feel safer and more secure.

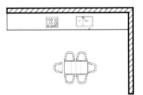

A kitchen in the common area is important. Running water, coffee maker, and utensils remind people of a cozy home.

Double doors serve as a zone where guards can question and filter out high-risk people. The intake room for the high-risk perpetrator is located right next to the guards.

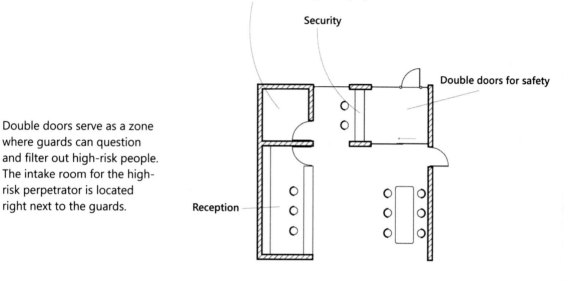

Intake room for high-risk perpetrator

Security

Double doors for safety

Reception

Some intake rooms are located next to the children's area so that parents don't lose sight of their children. The staff room next to the children's area can be a place where the staff monitors the corridor and the room.

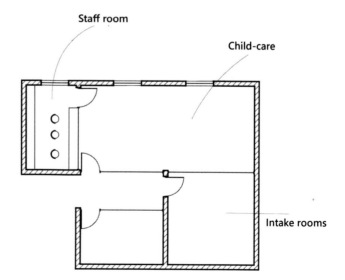

Staff room

Child-care

Intake rooms

Site Introduction

The students could choose from three sites that each represented different urban conditions, each roughly the same distance from City Hall and the Courthouse, frequently related destinations of the victims of domestic violence.

Site A

827 Chapel Street: A narrow slot site through a small existing building fronting on Chapel Street (between Orange and Federal Plaza) and running back to City Hall Square. The existing building could be engaged as part of the project or replaced. The site offers a more public entrance from Chapel Street versus a more private entrance off the interior court.

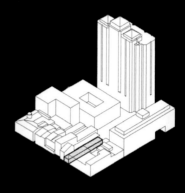

827 Chapel Street, New Haven

Site B

360 Orange Street: A vacant corner of Chapel Street and Orange Street, potentially the most active urban site of the three and most directly in its corner location, engaging the urban fabric of the city. As the largest of the three sites, some of the student work here included other relevant urban accessories to the program.

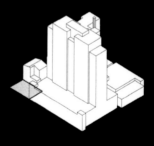

360 Orange Street, New Haven

Site C

107 Court Street: A narrow, more tucked-away street with smaller-scale buildings. The site runs back from Court Street through a narrow lot containing a residential-scale building to a mid-block parking lot into which the design could expand.

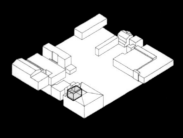

107 Court Street, New Haven

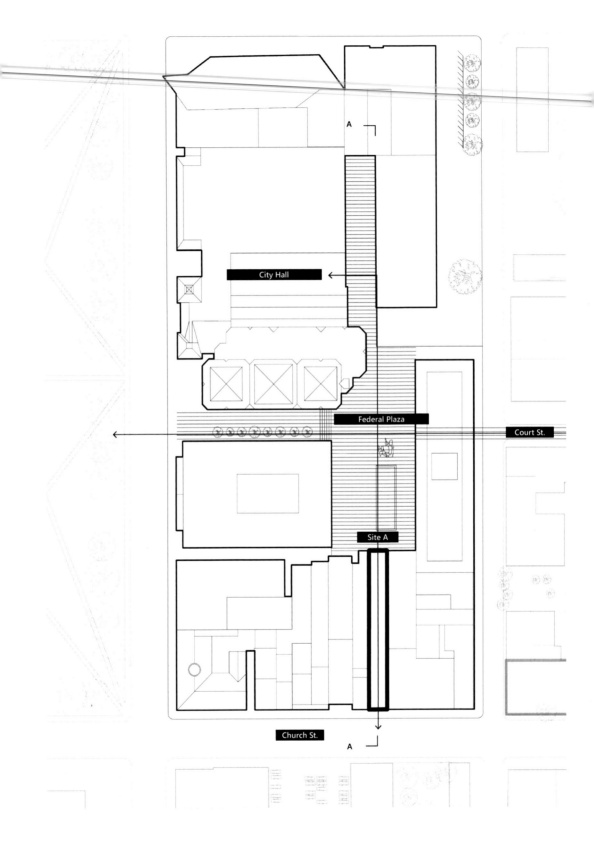

A

City Hall

Federal Plaza

Court St.

Site A

Church St.

A

Site A

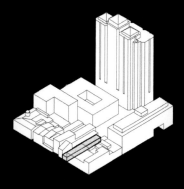

827 Chapel Street, New Haven

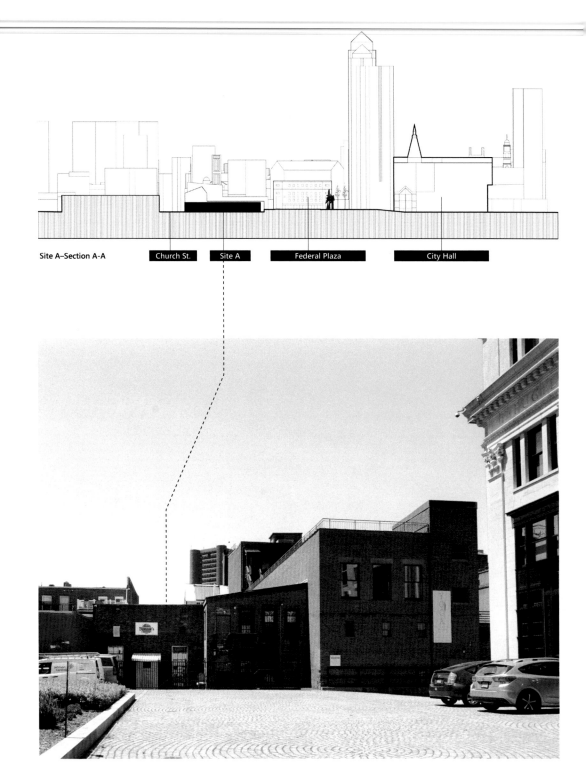

Site A–Section A-A | Church St. | Site A | Federal Plaza | City Hall

Photo taken from the Federal Plaza

Church St. elevation

Site A

Photo taken from Church St.

Curtain

Yue Geng

My project begins with a small corner behind a curtain to create an intimate atmosphere and respond in a flexible way to the different functional requirements in the building. The curtain corner could be opened and closed to expand or contract the space. The wraparound, individual, intimate spaces can open up to connect with multiple others in a sequence of connected spaces or create larger shared spaces.

The building is situated in a long narrow site between a street and an internal urban courtyard and can be entered from either end. From the street entrance, following the public circulation, one travels through the shared kitchen, past the family justice lecture hall, then to the gallery where survivors meet individual helpers, then finally to the rooftop cafe.

Prototype small corners with curtains

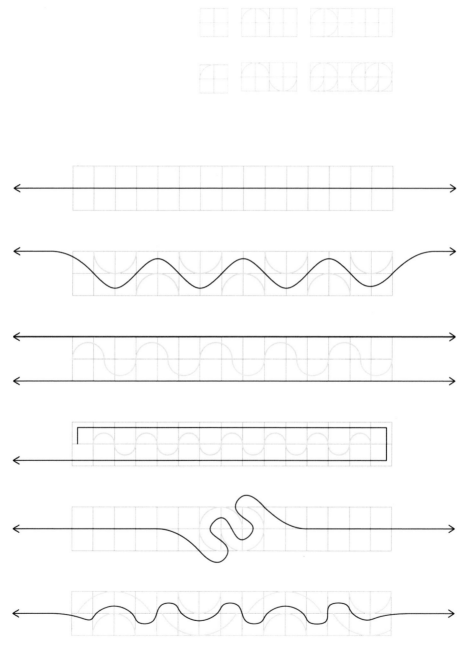

The interaction between corners and linear volume

Visitors can enter the building from either side. When the curtain closes, they become columns in the space. From the center, the visitor receives a safety security check to go upstairs. Then they come to the waiting area where they can experience the lecture or workshop. The corner rooms are the intake rooms. When the curtain closes, the entire floor could be used as a workshop space. On the upper floors, the curtain defines interview rooms, and the other spaces outside the curtain become work and public spaces that include a gallery, cafe, and kitchen. When the curtains are open, each floor is divided into more private space. When the curtains are closed, the spaces on different floors act as an extension into the public realm.

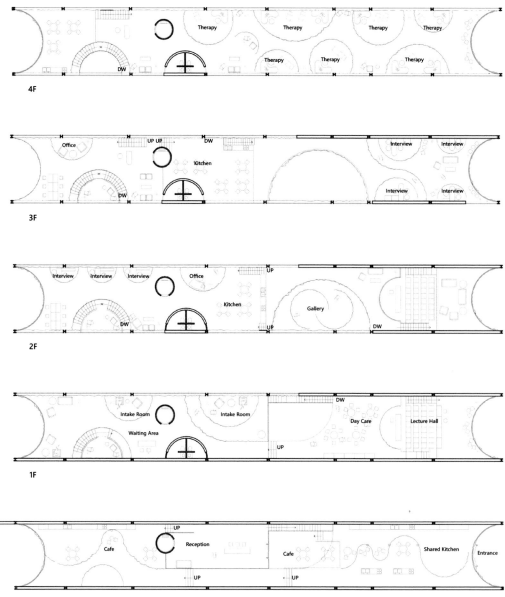

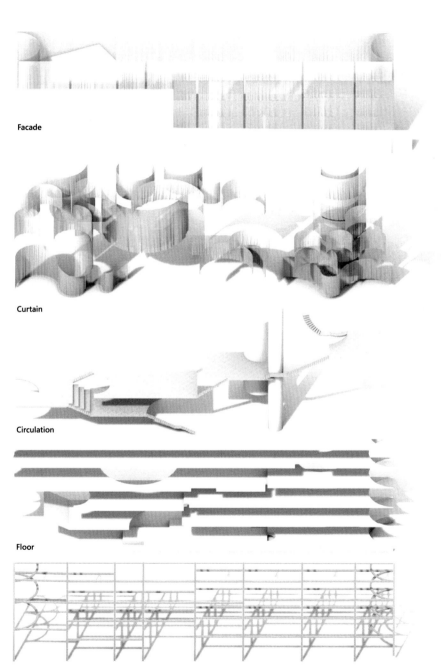

Facade

Curtain

Circulation

Floor

Structure

Section

Street

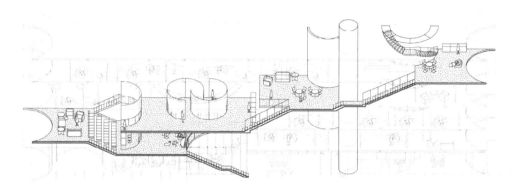

Main circulation

Movie corner

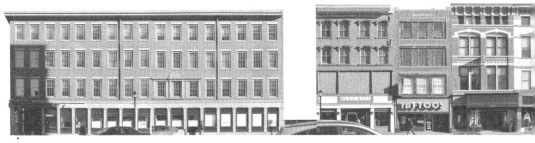

Street elevation

Gallery corner

Cafe terrace

Home Sweet Home

Ruike Liu

As Paola Serrecchia from the Hope Family Justice Center in New Haven said, "'Welcome home' is always the first thing I say when people come to the Family Justice Center." This project mimics the dimension and composition of spaces in a typical home—not big, but cozy. Furniture is fused into architectural structure, while building elements become occupiable. When people travel through the building, they can fit their body into the spaces, like a hideout or cozy corner. The design attempts to be an intimate temporary home where victims can share their stories.

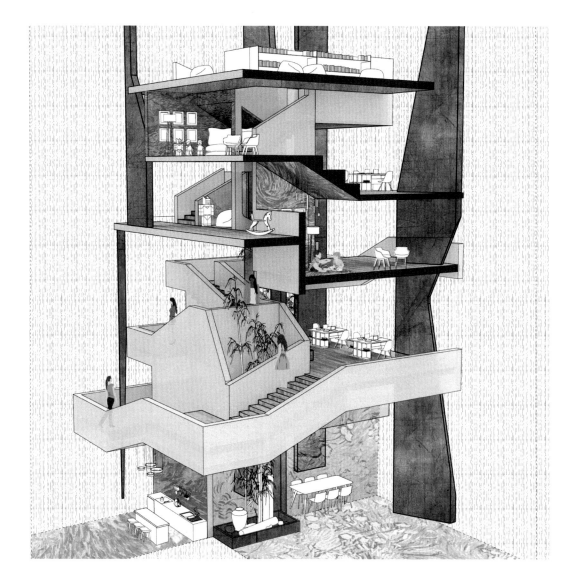

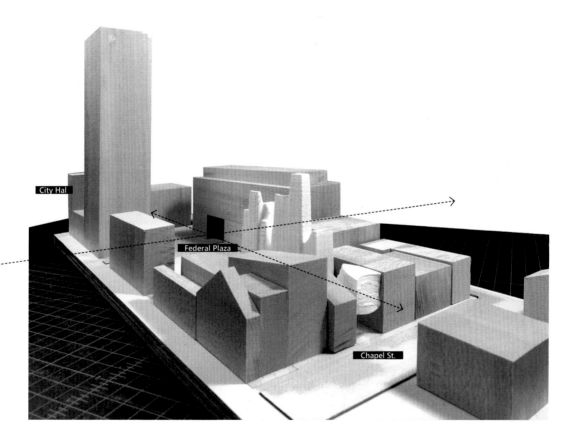

City Hall

Federal Plaza

Chapel St.

The site is a narrow linear slot linking Chapel Street and the Federal Plaza. City Hall is the first destination for most victims, many of whom will be instructed to visit Family Justice Center to process their cases. It seemed appropriate to allow victims two means of entering the building: 1) entry from the Plaza, a relatively private space; and 2) access from Chapel Street, a busier, more open street.

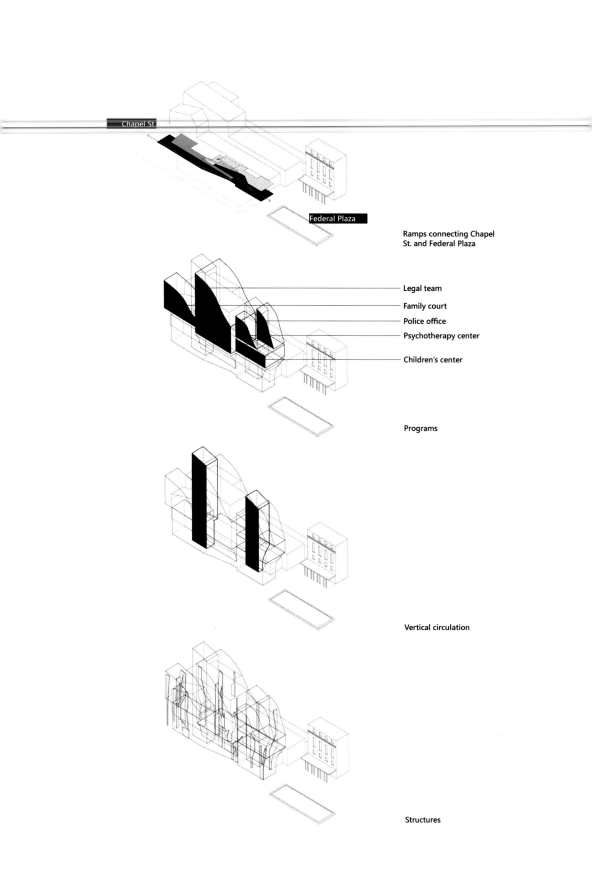

Chapel St.

Federal Plaza

Ramps connecting Chapel
St. and Federal Plaza

Legal team
Family court
Police office
Psychotherapy center

Children's center

Programs

Vertical circulation

Structures

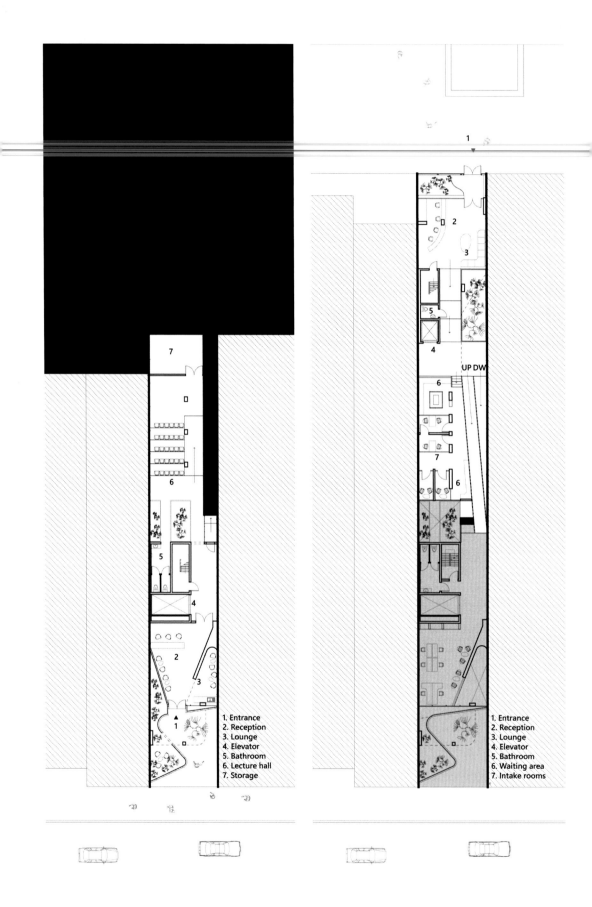

1. Entrance
2. Reception
3. Lounge
4. Elevator
5. Bathroom
6. Lecture hall
7. Storage

1. Entrance
2. Reception
3. Lounge
4. Elevator
5. Bathroom
6. Waiting area
7. Intake rooms

UP DW

View from the ramp

Waiting area in front of the intake rooms

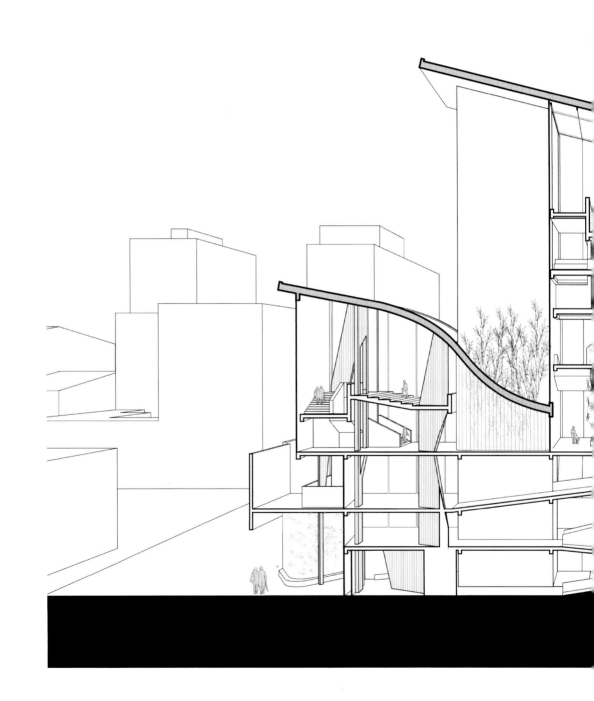

Perspectival Section

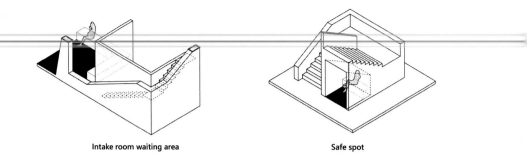

Intake room waiting area

Safe spot

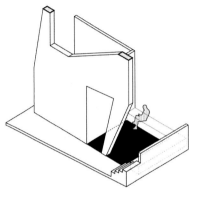

Intake room waiting area

Interview room

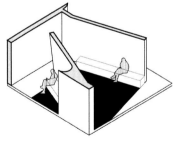

Reception lounge

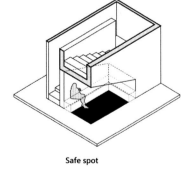

Safe spot

People feel safe when they are not visible and are able to supervise others. "Safe spots" are being created everywhere in the project. These spaces are semi-open. The equivocality provides liminal zones for temporary escape.

Child-care area

Survival group meeting room

Mediator

Robin Hengyuan Yang

Trauma makes people feel like somebody else, or feel like nobody. To overcome trauma, one needs help to get back in touch with one's body, mind, and senses.

The new building could be a mediator between the world and the body. The sequence of curtain walls creates layers of space interweaving courtyards, public space, and intimate service rooms, bringing light, air, and intimacy to every visitor.

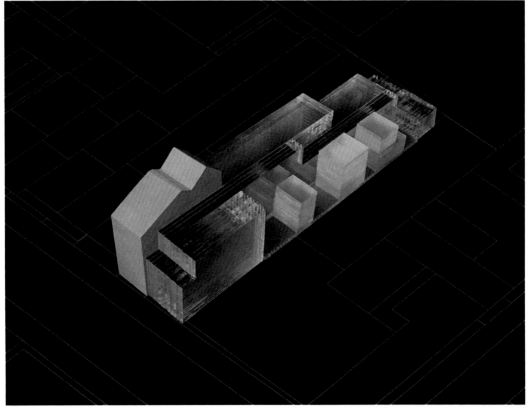

Concept model - volume and courtyard

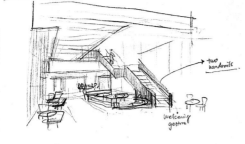

Waiting area

Reception

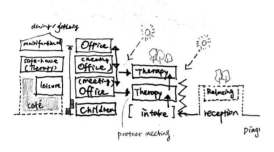

Programs in section

Diagrammatic section

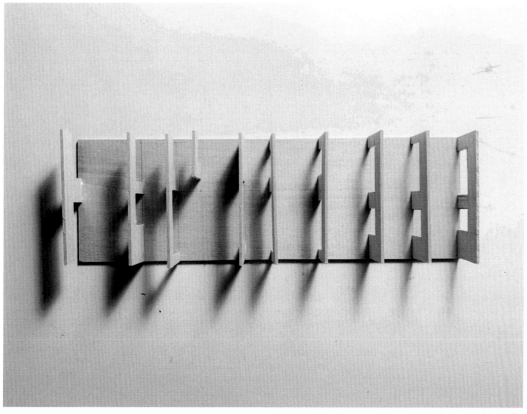

Concept model—rhythm

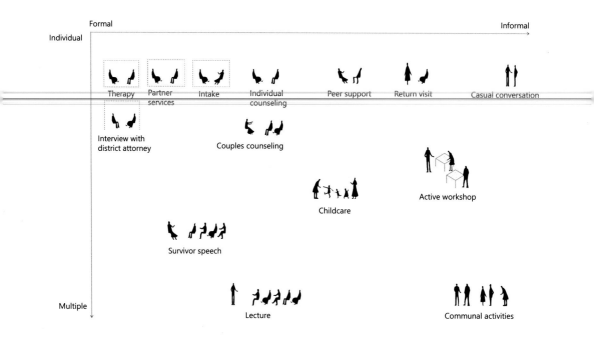

Formal → Informal

Individual

Therapy | Partner services | Intake | Individual counseling | Peer support | Return visit | Casual conversation

Interview with district attorney

Couples counseling

Childcare

Active workshop

Survivor speech

Multiple

Lecture

Communal activities

Different types of communication

Study model

Victims brought to FJC by police or by social worker from the courthouse

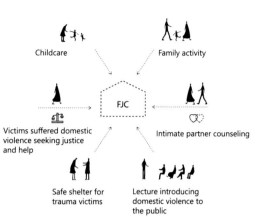

Childcare

Family activity

Victims suffered domestic violence seeking justice and help

FJC

Intimate partner counseling

Safe shelter for trauma victims

Lecture introducing domestic violence to the public

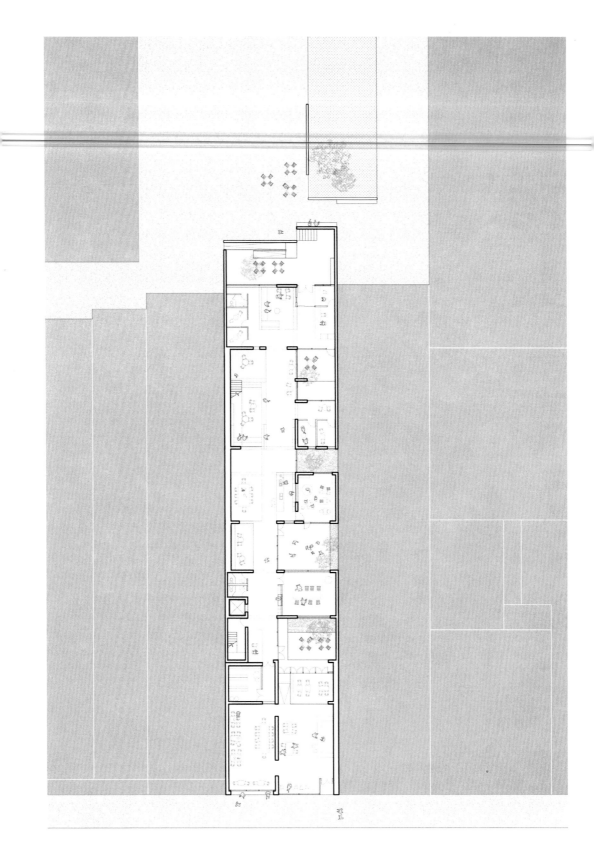

Ground-floor plan

View of the reception area

View of the cafe

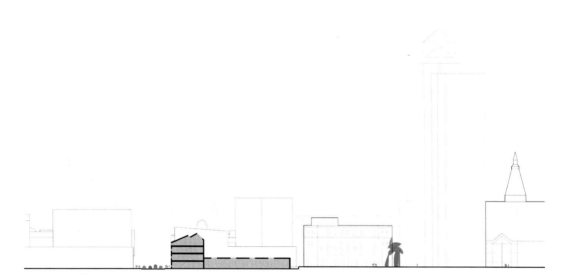

Original site section

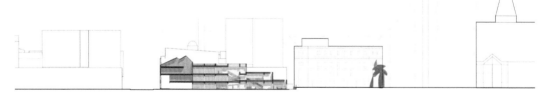

New site section

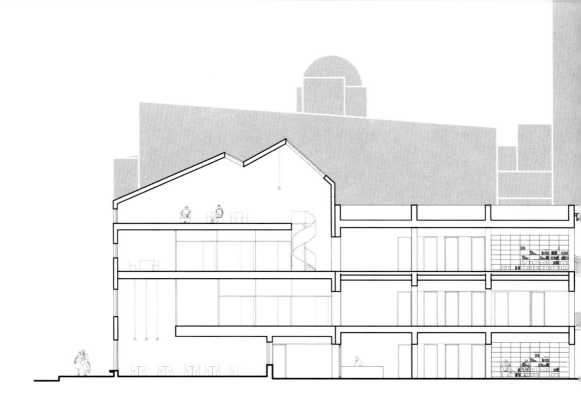

Section

View of the kitchen

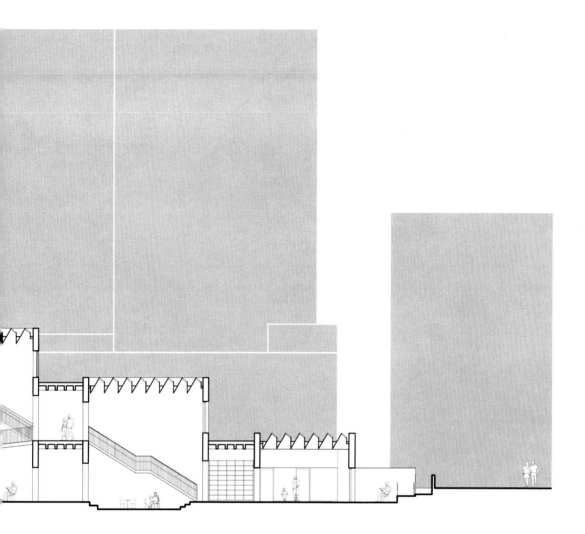

View of the library

The Passageway

Alexander Velaise

This project, The Passageway, centers around transitioning a domestic violence victim past a state of surviving to a state of thriving. Equal importance is given to both the experience of the staff who support the victim's transition and the children who absorb the trauma of their parents. A linear site that extends from the quiet Federal Plaza, where a victim can enter safely, to busy commercial Chapel Street, acts as a liminal zone that begins to normalize the concept of family justice in the community.

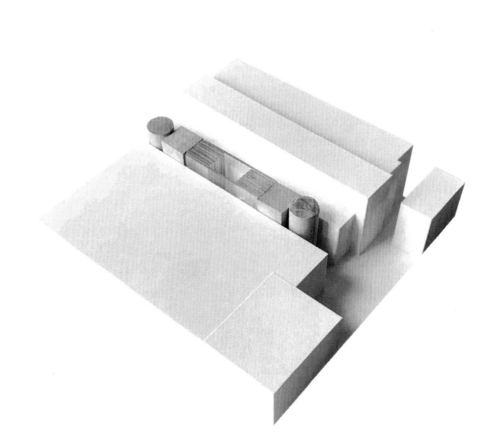

Concept massing model: Two concrete zones act as liminal gateways to an interior atrium.

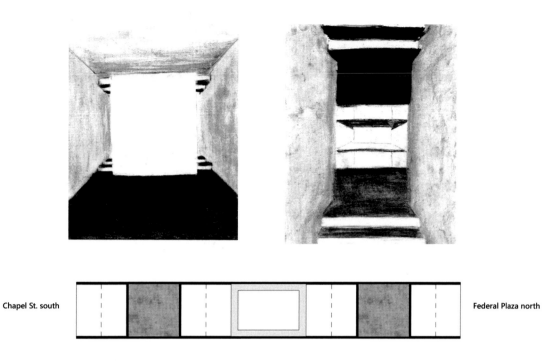

Chapel St. south   Federal Plaza north

Conceptual gateways diagram: Two ramped cores act as gates to the interior courtyard, surrounded by the programmatic moments of interface between staff and client.

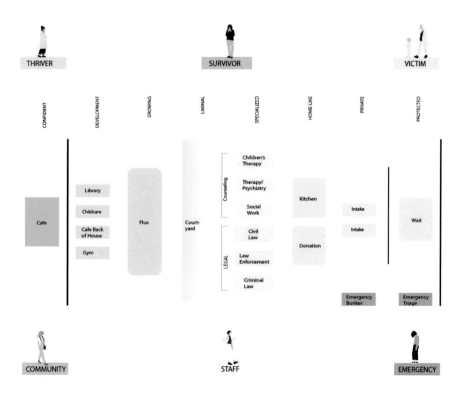

Programmatic flow: People move through and stop at different points that overlap one another.

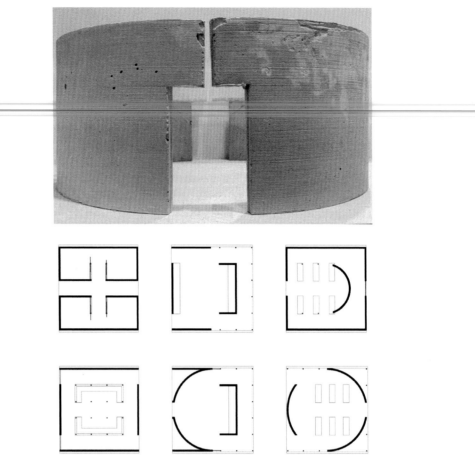

Geometric plan development: The interior logic of the interstitial space is rooted in cloister-like circles and squares.

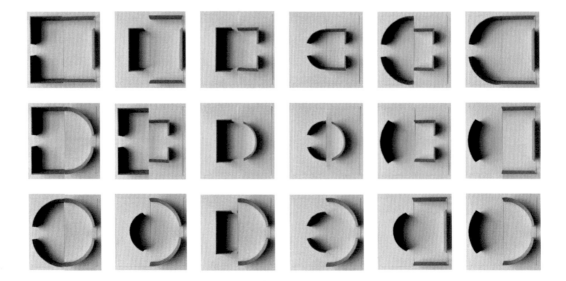

Geometric plan iteration: These geometries react to the cores and change to accommodate their intended programs.

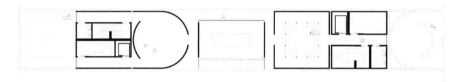

Roof floor

F5 plan

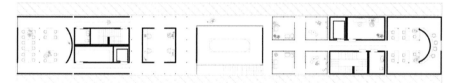

F4 plan

F2 plan

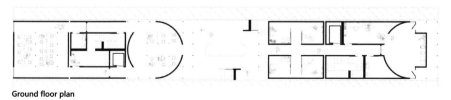

Ground floor plan

Plans: Users are nudged and nurtured through their intended transitions
using simple sculptural elements that inspire introspection and meditation.

Longitudinal section: Ramps create sectional hierarchy, and circulations show
the nesting and mixing of users between the north and south structures.

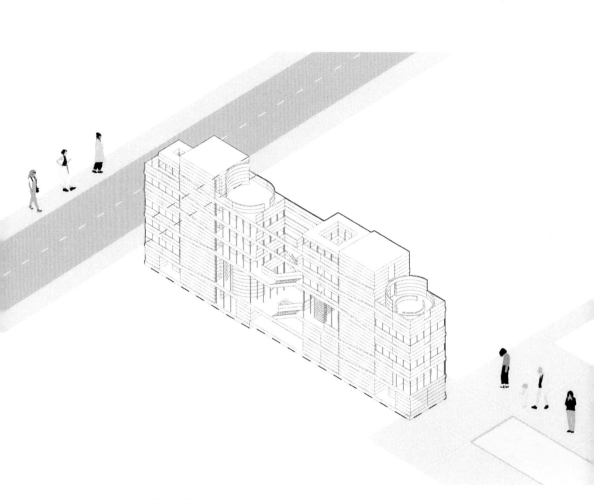

Axonometric drawing: The building has inputs and outputs that guide people
along an introspective journey, from victim to survivor, in order to thrive.

Exterior perspective: Vew from Chapel Street looking into the community cafe.

Interior perspective: View as a victim enters into the sculptural moment of uplifting and mixing.

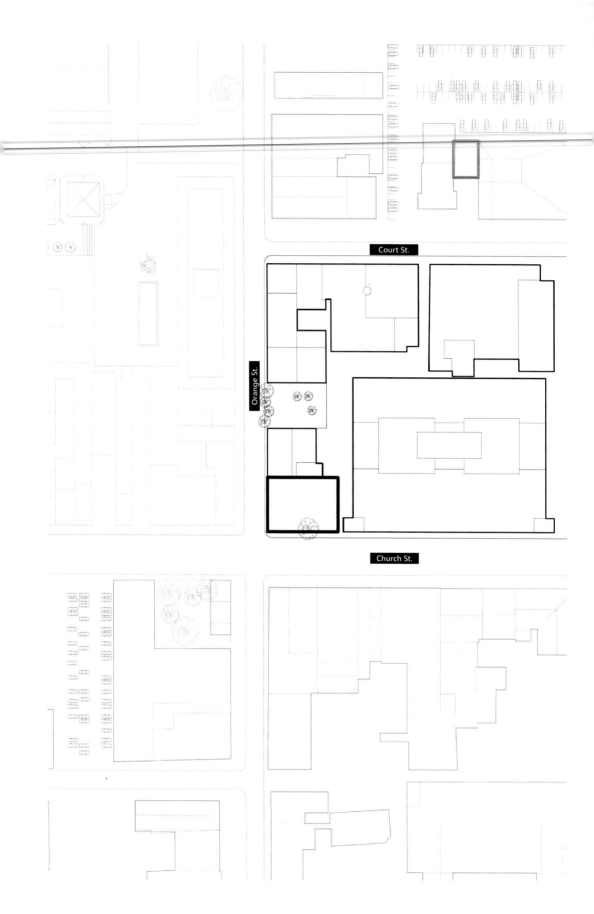

Court St.

Orange St.

Church St.

Site B

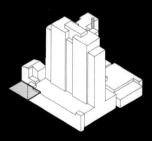

360 Orange Street, New Haven

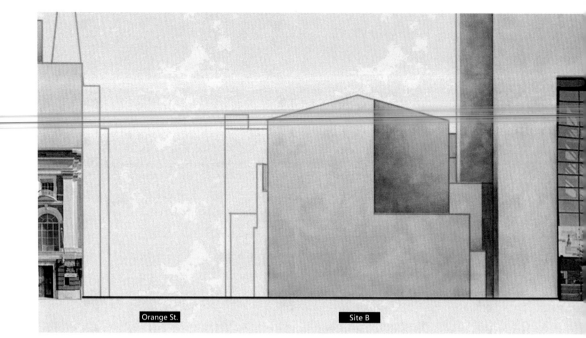

Church St. elevation

Photo taken from Orange Street

Photo taken from Church St.

Transitional Space

Shuchen Dong

This project, Transitional Space, probes prototypes of spaces that make people who are enduring stress feel safe, and where they can sense that everything is under control. The methodology is to develop prototypes that adapt to a hierarchy of interrelated spaces, moving from public to private. When a person wanders inside the building, there are no sharp corners or unknown spaces. They can always sense the spatial orientation, feel protected, and directly observe what is happening.

Images	Analysis	Seeds	Proto space

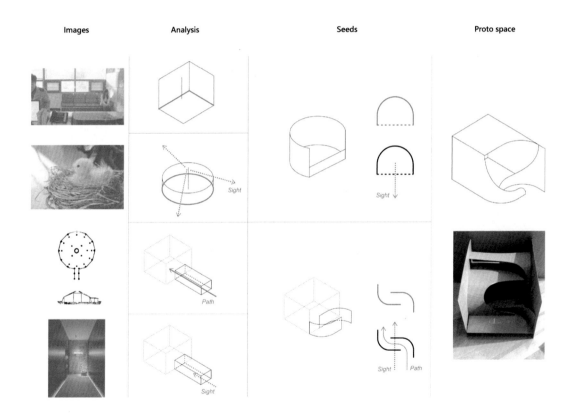

View from Chapel Street.

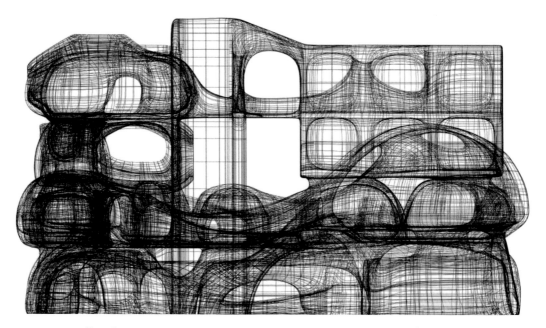

"Burrow"

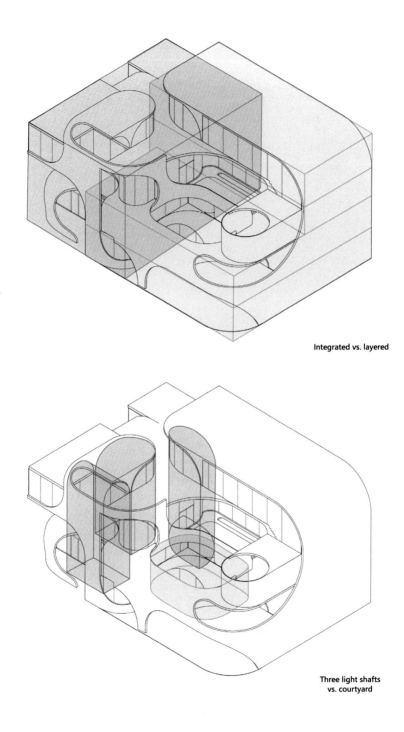

Integrated vs. layered

Three light shafts
vs. courtyard

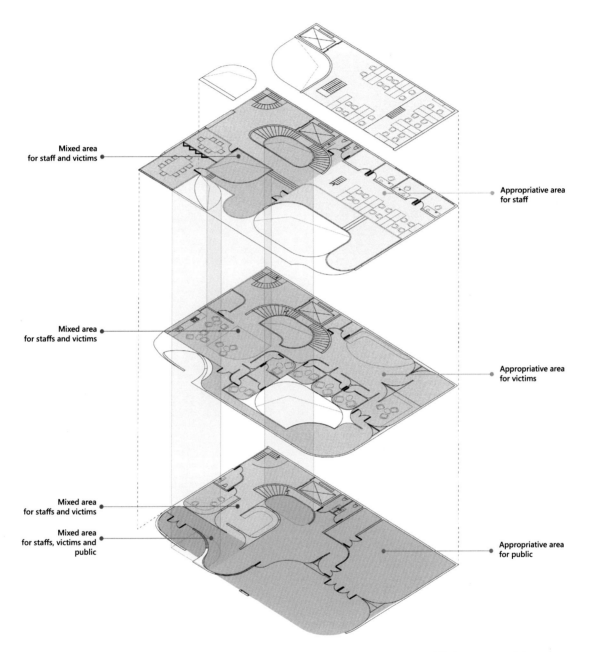

Mixed area
for staff and victims

Appropriative area
for staff

Mixed area
for staffs and victims

Appropriative area
for victims

Mixed area
for staffs and victims

Mixed area
for staffs, victims and
public

Appropriative area
for public

Mixed area vs. appropriative area

69

Elevation

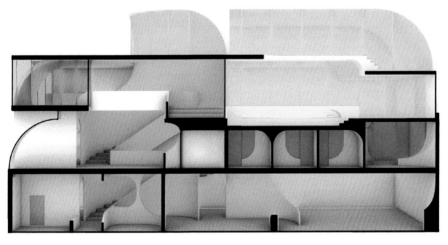

Section

Section

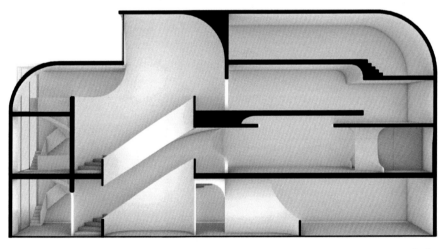

Section

Reconciliation

Qizhen Tang

This proposal, Reconciliation, explores the subtle balance between the Family Justice Center's "inward" qualities and role addressing serious social issues of domestic violence and sometimes crimes, and its "outward" qualities as a civic center serving as an open shelter for mutual assistance, public education, and other community activities. Two basic thoughts guide the design process: the first is how the space could be organized and shaped into a diversity of "humane" qualities to fulfill the different needs of multiple programs under a dominant, even mechanic, order of scale and structure; the second is how the spatial organization would match human movement and activities in the architecture to create a smooth "sequence" of both services/programs and spatial experience.

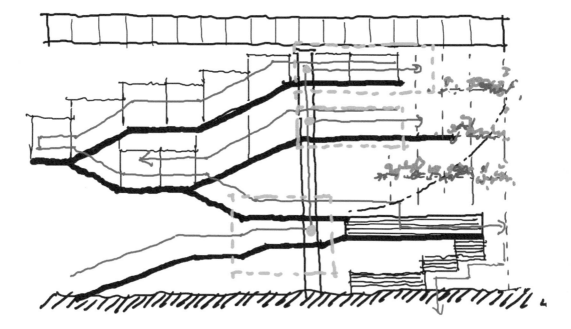

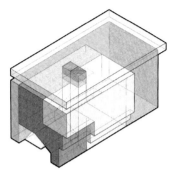

Two interlocking volumes, for public/open programs and private/intimate programs, along with the wrapping as a third conceptual mass.

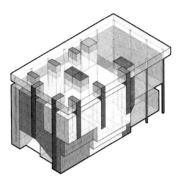

The embedding of structural and spatial modules (light-shaft-box trusses as suspension rods) that "anchor" the basic compositional volumes of the facility.

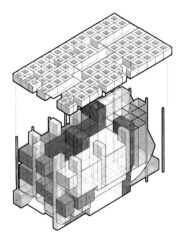

Unified rooms of the main service area (intake rooms, consultant rooms, etc.), single volume of the offices, and the narrow light atriums, which serve as partitions between the two volumes.

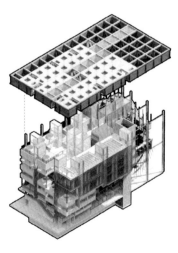

Materialized interpretation of the main components: main service areas, staff offices, public ground floors, and the wood "wrapping" around the solid volumes.

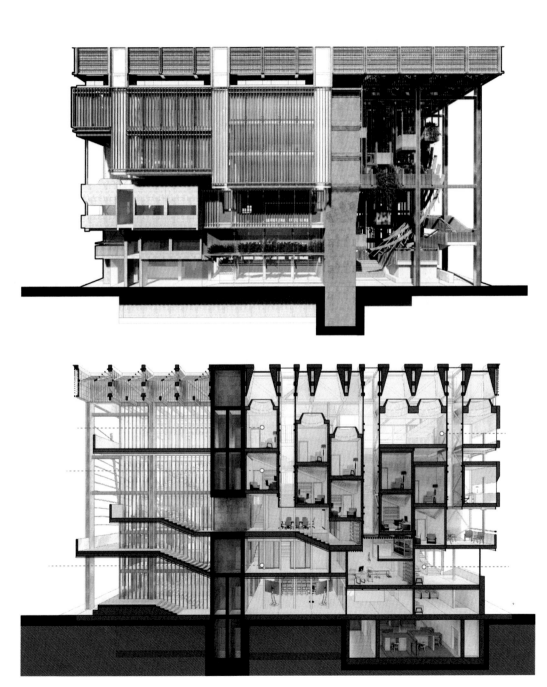

Elevation and section

Standing at the intermediate level looking
at the upper stairs with initial intake rooms,
accompanied by a series of lower stairs with
additional service rooms.

Descending stairs

The common area located between the service part and the office/staff part. It is also a
main entrance to the semi-outdoor "garden"
with seats and mini-plantations.

Common area

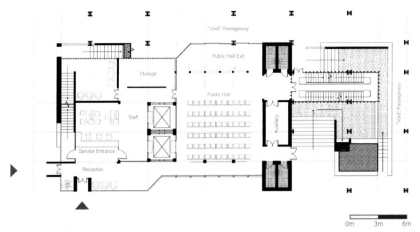

Ground floor

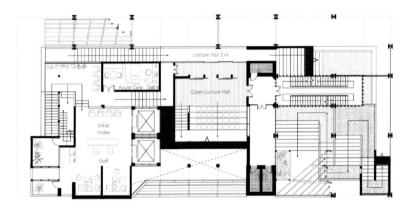

Second floor

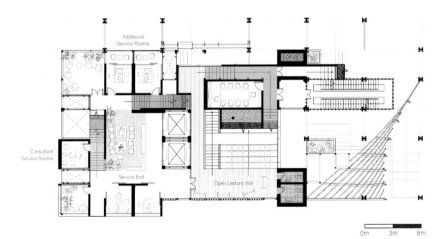

Third floor

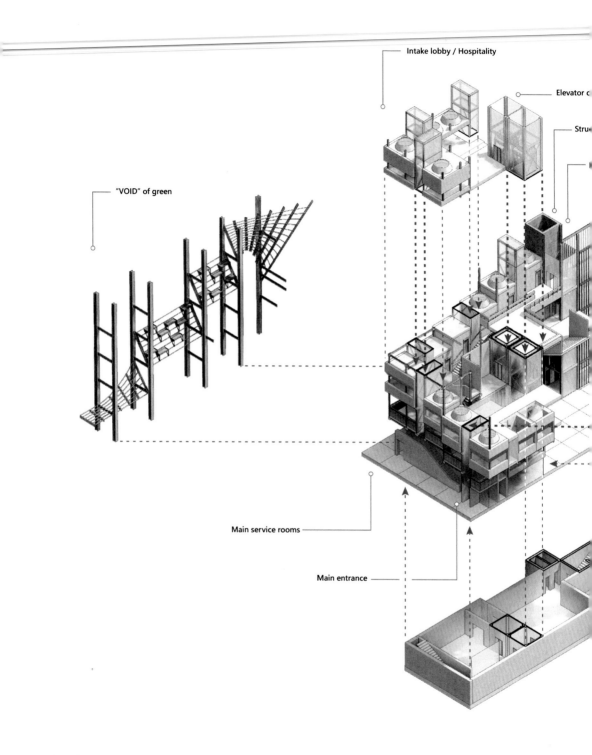

"VOID" of green

Intake lobby / Hospitality

Elevator c

Stru

Main service rooms

Main entrance

Composition

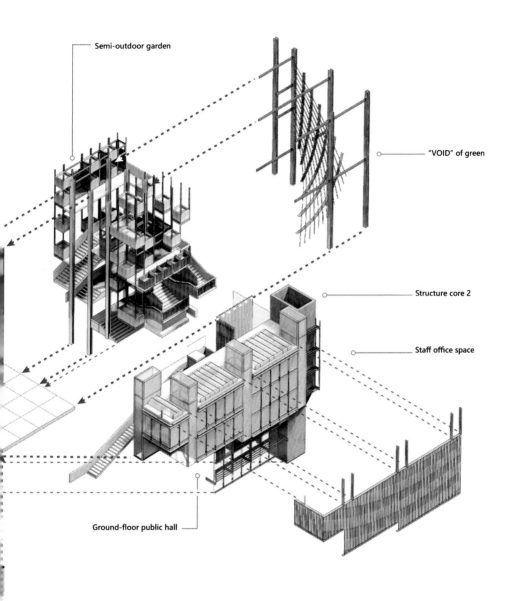

Semi-outdoor garden

"VOID" of green

Structure core 2

Staff office space

Ground-floor public hall

Multifunction basement

Atrium

Daoru Wang

As shelters become the places of nightmares, and as those who should protect victims become perpetrators, more and more people stand to suffer from domestic violence. Undoubtably, the victims face challenges even when—and if—the perpetrators stop their abuses. Along with physical and psychological healing, most will face further significant emotional and financial challenges.

This project, The Atrium, focuses on the design of a helping center for those victims who experience domestic violence, with the primary goal being to create a space where the victims can get treatment from social workers of different disciplines. This project considers victims' need for softness and warmth. The cave-like entrance to this facility provides a sense of safety while protecting the victims' privacy; simultaneously, the atrium space allows building users to enjoy private outdoor time while bringing soft light into the interior. Curved surfaces and natural light enhance the spaces and project design.

Additional programs are introduced into the building complex, including temporary housing units and an educational center, to assist the victims and help them to acquire useful skills in their recovery.

View of the entrance

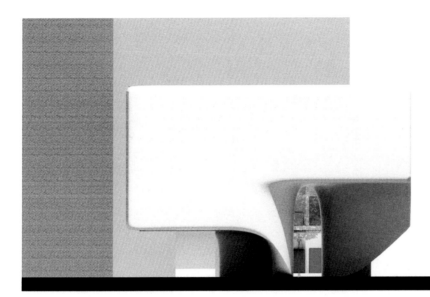

Elevation

Section

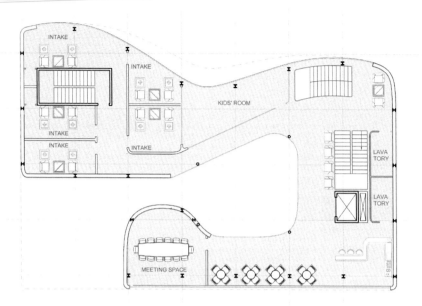

FIRST FLOOR 16"

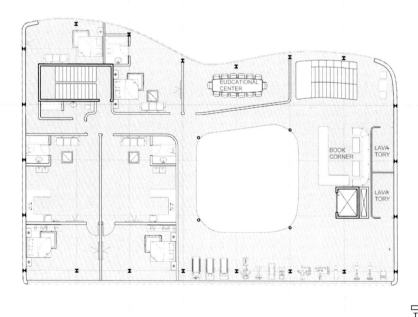

THIRD FLOOR 16"

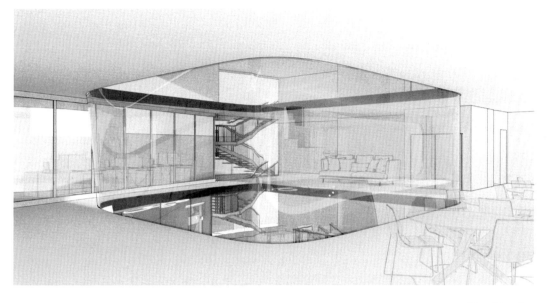

View of the atrium

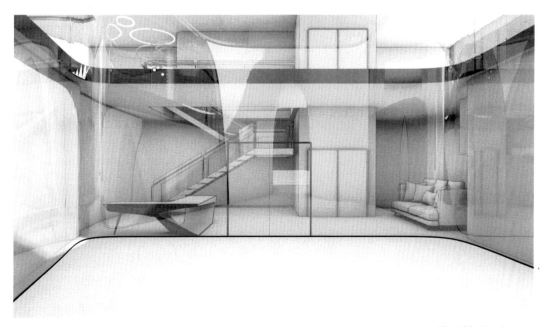

View of the interview room

Choreography

Shiqi Li

Surviving trauma is a winding and iterative journey, in which people alternate between mutable physical and mental needs. In this project, the interplay between different spaces led to permeable interfaces, fluid circulation, and ambiguous boundaries. A field of wandering paths permeate the building block, offering a spectrum of different enclosures and connections to give people various choices to join or withdraw, to wander or pass through, or to proceed at their own pace.

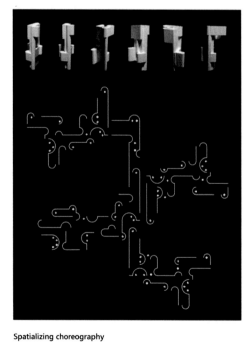

Spatializing choreography

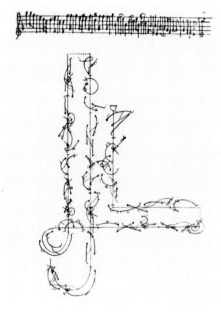

Raoul-Auger Feuillet, *Choregraphie*, 1701

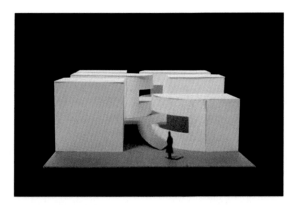

Liminal space conceptual model

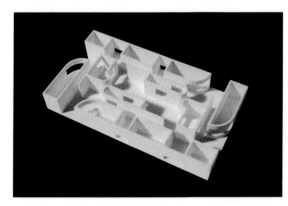

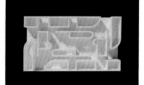

Floor plan prototype

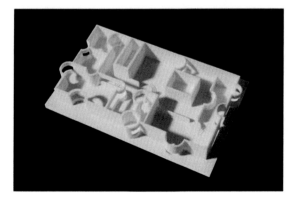

Floor plan prototype

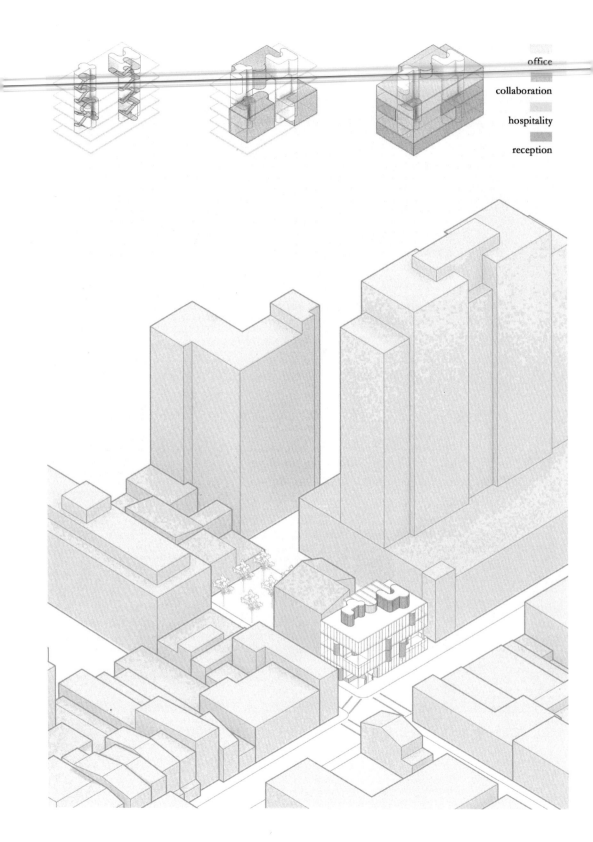

office

collaboration

hospitality

reception

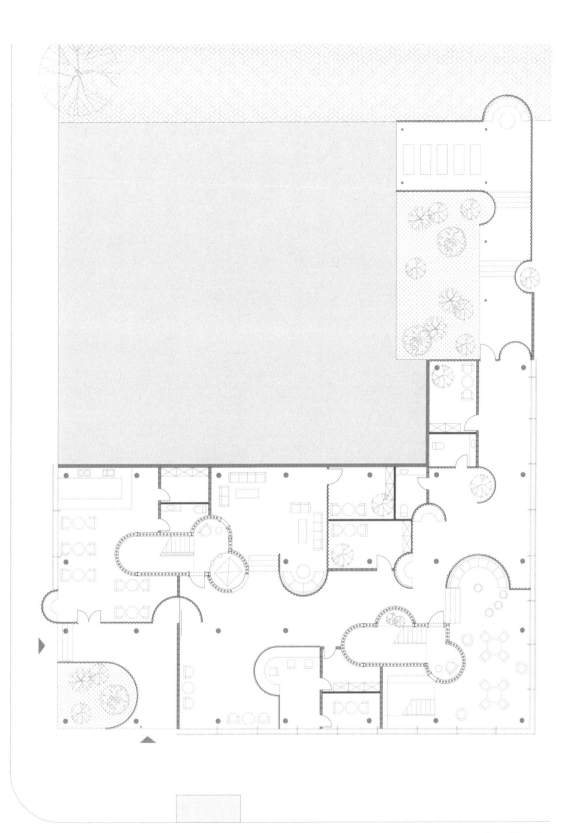

Ground-floor plan

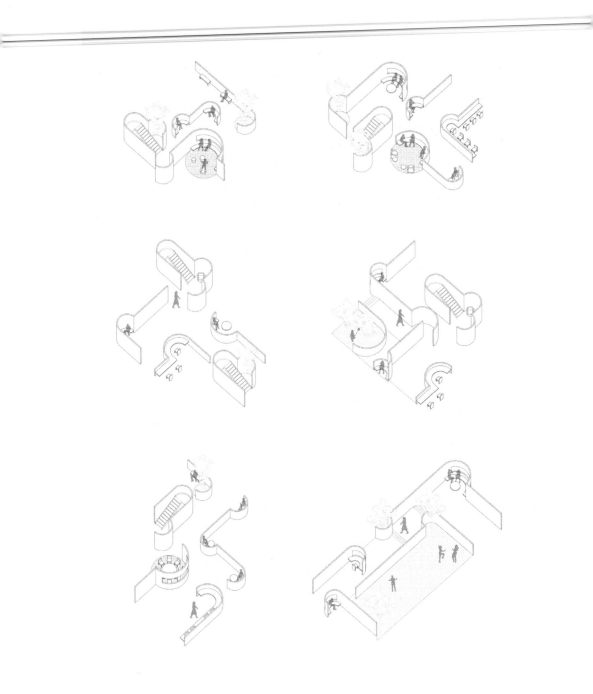

Conceptual archetype study: Developing an architectural language that divides and connects various activities

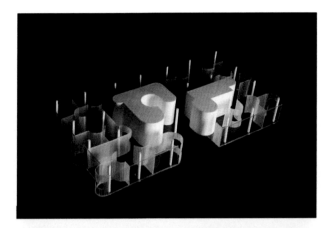

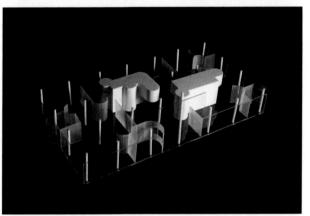

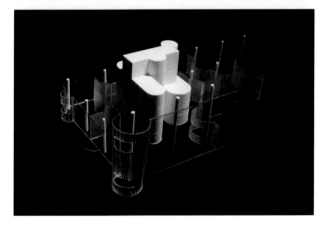

Spatial transparency study: Discussing spatial hierarchy and sense of direction

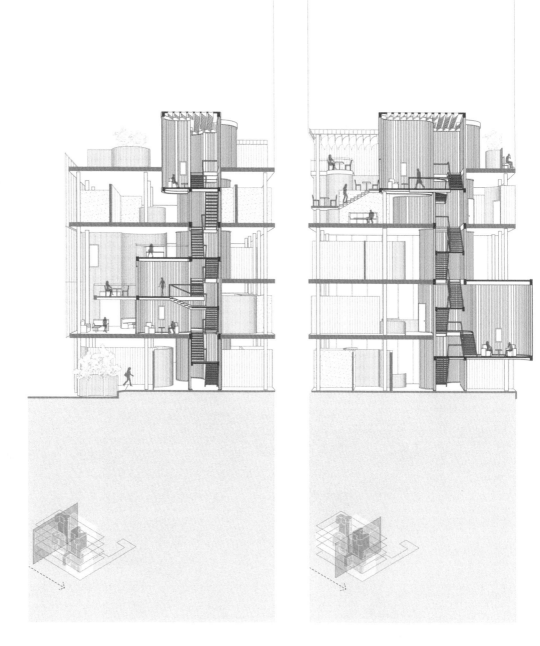

Section

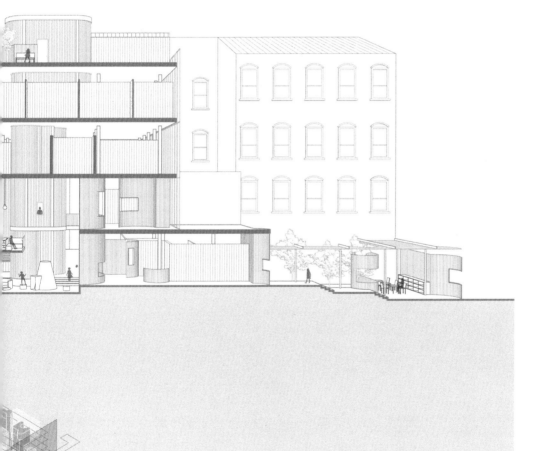

In-between space: Choreography of fluid and rhythmic movement

Functional space: Wrapped and permeable spatial nodes for pause

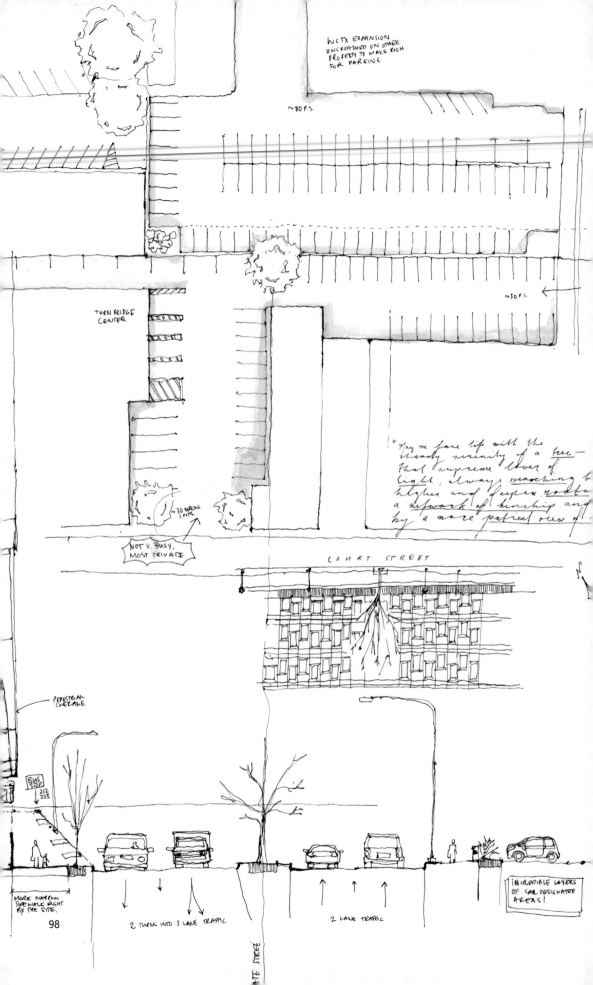

WCTX EXPANSION
ENCROACHED ON OTHER
PROPERTY TO MAKE ROOM
FOR PARKING

~80 P.S.

~30 P.S.

TURN BRIDGE
CENTER

→ 30 PARKING
1 PITS.

NOT V. BUSY,
MOST PRIVATE

"May me face life with the
steady serenity of a tree —
that supreme lover of
light, always reaching to
higher and deeper roots
a network of kinship and
by a more patient view of

COURT STREET

PEDESTRIAN
OVERLANE

BUS
STOP
212
213

MORE NARROW
SIDEWALK RIGHT
BY THE SITE.

2 TURNS INTO 3 LANE TRAFFIC.

2 LANE TRAFFIC

INCREDIBLE LAYERS
OF CAR DESIGNATED
AREAS!

Site C

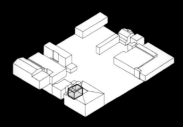

107 Court Street, New Haven

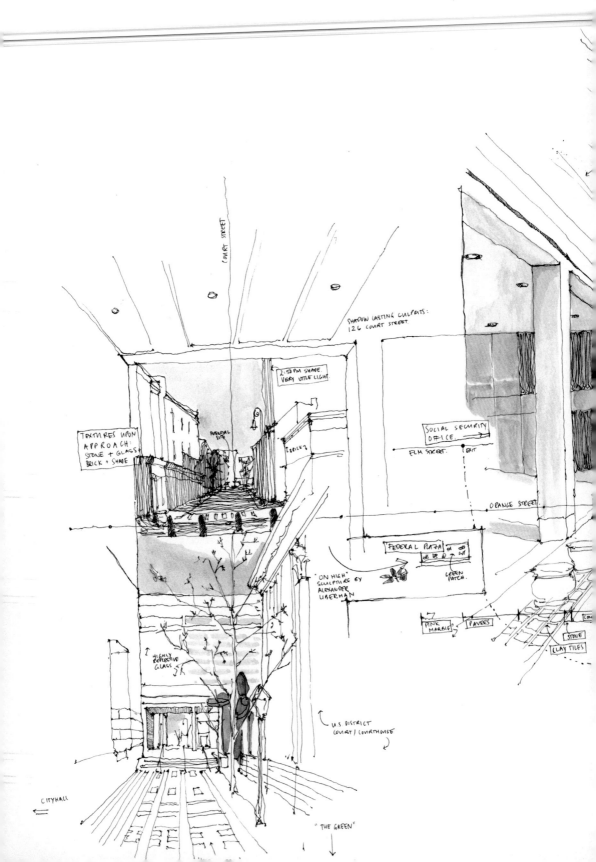

COURT STREET

SHADOW CASTING CULPRITS:
126 COURT STREET.

2:50 PM SHADE
VERY LITTLE LIGHT.

TEXTURES UPON
APPROACH:
STONE + GLASS +
BRICK + SHADE

SUNDIAL LIFE

BRICK

SOCIAL SECURITY
OFFICE.

ELM STREET.   EXIT

ORANGE STREET.

FEDERAL PLAZA

GREEN
PATCH.

"ON HIGH"
SCULPTURE BY
ALEXANDER
LIBERMAN

PINE
MARBLE   PAVERS

STONE
CLAY TILES

HIGHLY
REFLECTIVE
GLASS

U.S. DISTRICT
COURT / COURTHOUSE

CITYHALL
←

"THE GREEN"
↓

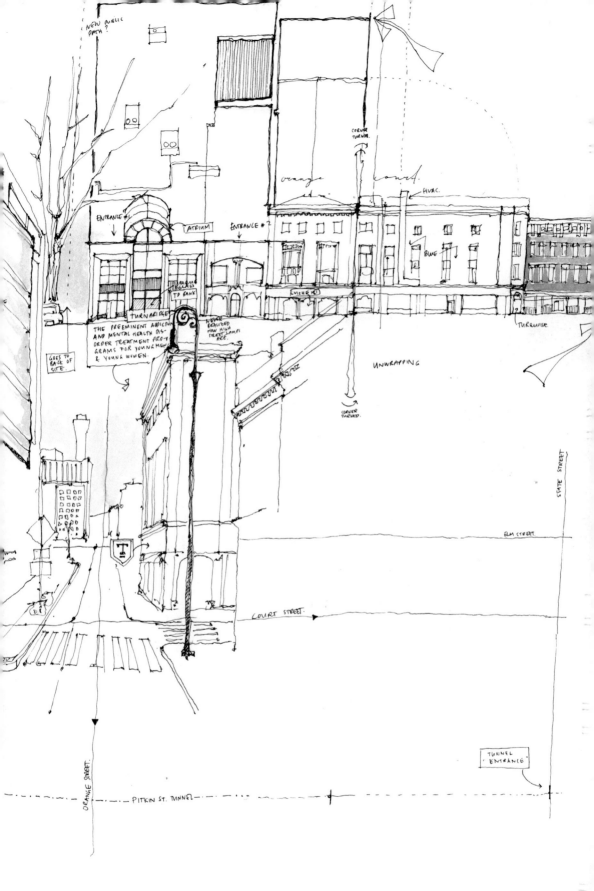

Site analysis, Rhea Schmid

Photo taken from Court Street

Photo taken from parking lot

Embodied

Rhea Schmid

Victims of domestic violence embody their trauma. Though the wounds are not always visible, they can begin to manifest physically: in posture, in a tendency to avoid eye contact, and in an inability to feel pain or even identify it. As designers of space, and curators of sensory experiences, how can we even begin to talk about embodying space when we are working with people who, due to trauma, have difficulties substantiating their own body?

"Embodied" proposes that such a reconnection is possible through architecture. The process is action-oriented, broken down into three verbs: to arrive, to address, to attune. "To arrive" speaks of a conscious decision to seek help. A looped entrance allows victims to slip discreetly into an entry courtyard, while their path is the same as that used by staff, ensuring a dignified yet secure arrival. "To address" understands that

needs must be met in every stage of life. Intake rooms are made available throughout the center for reassessment. And "to attune" celebrates the desire to engage with life itself. A "donation runway," where victims can pick out and parade a new change of clothes, looks over the office spaces below. These three verbs help recognize that victims can transition in and out of the states of victim, survivor, and thriver (three steps of the healing journey). It is the spatial transition that is critical—the realization of a "delta," and therefore one's own spatial substance. "Embodied" is rooted in a desire and responsibility to acknowledge, understand, and address both collective and individual needs. This project has underscored the importance of incorporating those needs and integrating realities like trauma into the design process, no matter how complex.

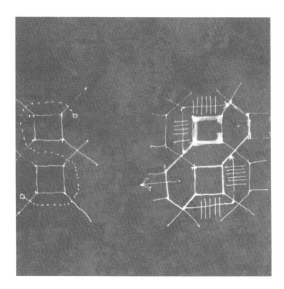

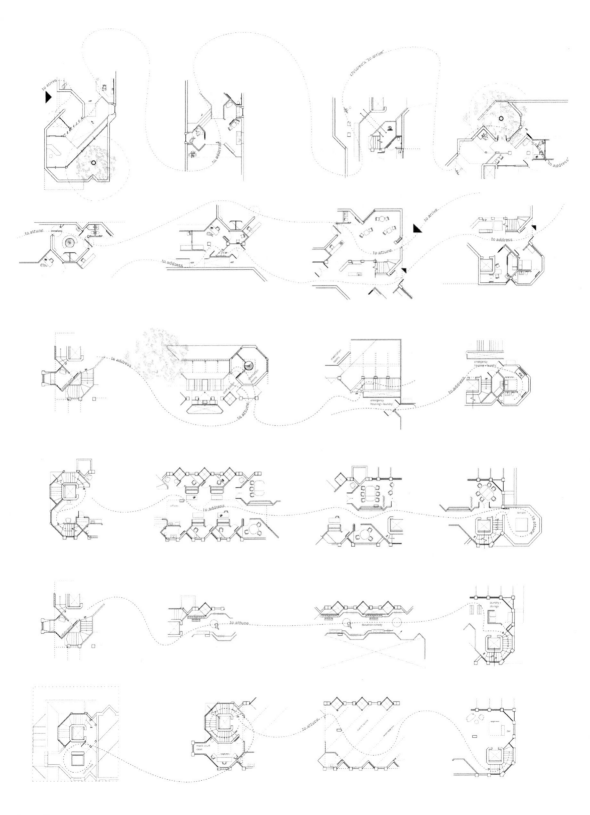

Plan studies

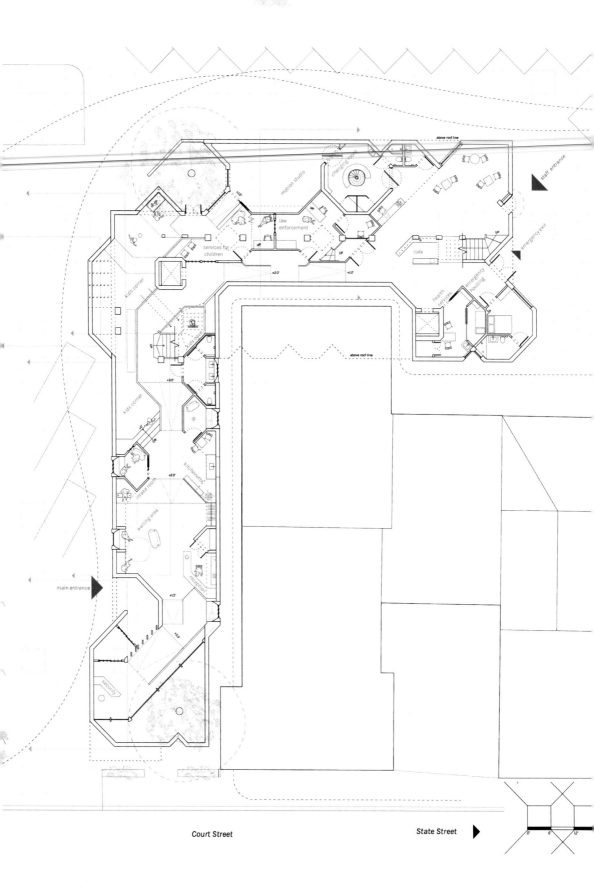

Within the plan (labels):

above roof line

motion studio

changing

staff entrance

law enforcement

services for children

cafe

emergency exit

kids corner

health services

emergency housing

above roof line

+3.0'

kids corner

kitchenette

+2.0'

intake room

waiting area

reception

+1.5'

+0.5'

main entrance

security

Court Street

State Street

0'   6'   12'

Ground-floor plan

Section

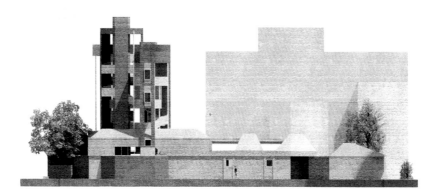

Elevation

View of the entrance

Perspectival section

Re-Familiar

Smit Patel

The project creates a safe haven for the victims of domestic violence on their journey towards becoming "Thrivers." To create this safe haven, the users should have a sense of ownership over the project, their own small-scale urban environment, which would be a city with different partner services coming together. Architecture is a language to re-familiarize the body to the urban and the domestic, with elements of surprise and moments of recognition.

Model—Elevation

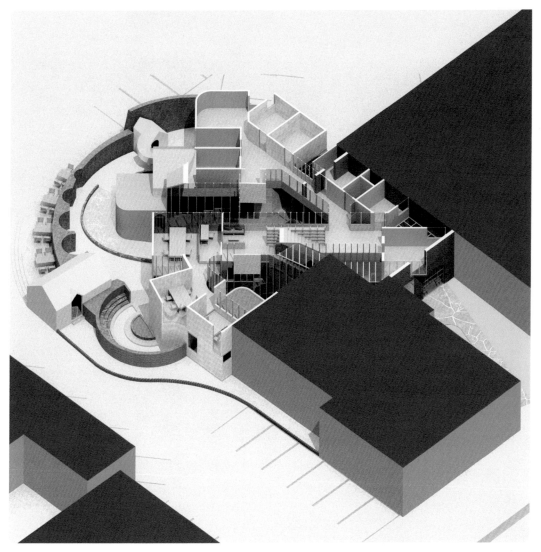

Level two axonometric drawing

Model site plan

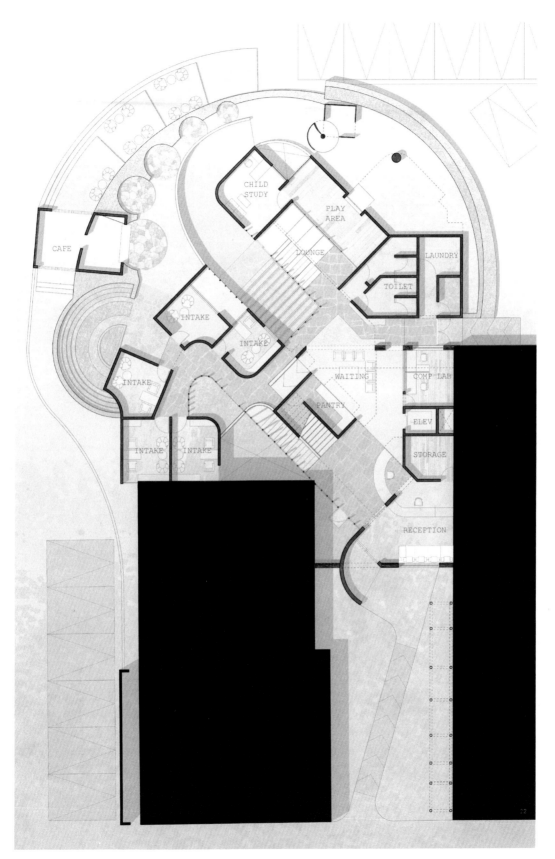

Ground-floor plan

Model elevation

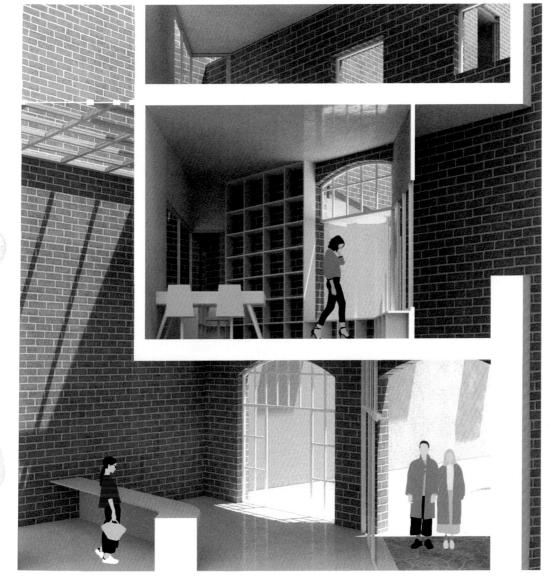

Section

Interior rendering of the indetween space

Interior rendering of the waiting area

Design for Care

Rhea Schmid

Family Justice Center acknowledges domestic violence as a public health crisis "of epidemic proportions."[1] As both a civic establishment and a resource for victims, these centers coalesce multiple avenues of assistance, ranging from medical to legal to psychological. We learned that the basic structure of the program includes a reception area with intake rooms for initial interviewing, office spaces for professional guidance, spaces for the clients' children to play and meet with child specialists, and multipurpose spaces for workshops and events, but can also include a range of additional spaces for clinics, emergency housing, and other services.

Throughout the semester we met with professionals, visited American and Dutch Family Justice Centers, and worked closely with BHcare's The Umbrella Center for Domestic Violence Services to learn from them and to present our proposals for a Family Justice Center in New Haven. In tandem, we continued to unpack the rich architectural themes derived from the meaningful program. The program could best be conceived as a series of contradicting dualities—the civic vs. the discreet, autonomy vs. coexistence, innocence vs. violence, and immediate needs vs. future aspirations. These dualities were explored, blurred, and broken down through model making, drawing, and literature, where "liminal space," "ambiguity," and "vulnerability" became very real architectural concepts with which to contend.

Each student focused on quite different design approaches, which resulted in a collection of interesting and varied projects. Some of us researched the internal processes and workings of existing Family Justice Centers to derive new spatial sequences; some embraced an appropriate urban form and infused it with program; and others focused on human narratives to help generate meaningful space. Though the processes and expressions vary, it is safe to say that we all walked away from this experience with a deeper understanding of the real and debilitating effects of trauma that result from domestic abuse and violence. Trauma is complex, highly contextual, and systemic, and cannot be ignored in the design process. The current state of the world is the result of a society that failed to design with those most traumatized in mind. Here's to design rooted in hope, what's right and good, and a desire to create architecture that serves even the most vulnerable members of our community.

1. Rachel Louise Snyder, *No Visible Bruises: What We Don't Know About Domestic Violence Can Kill Us.* (New York: Bloomsbury Publishing, 2019).

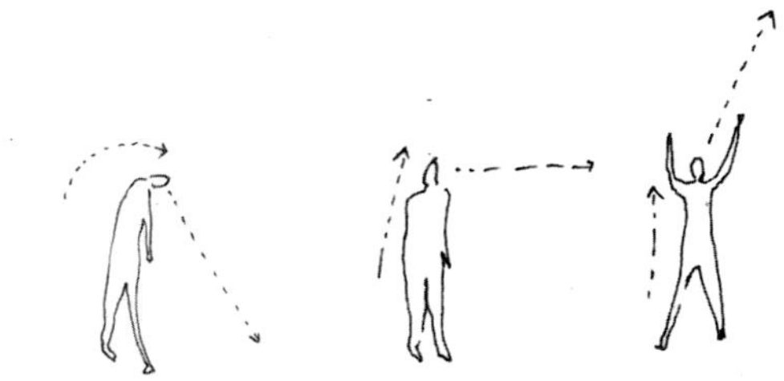

Image Credits

Cover image	Shuchen Dong
P1	Shuchen Dong
P4	Alexander Velaise
P4	Daoru Wang
P9	Shuchen Dong
P10 top	Fig.1, Edward Hopper, *Rooms by the Sea*. Courtesy of the Yale Gallery, New Haven (https://artgallery.yale.edu/collections/objects/52939)
P10 bottom	Fig.2, Joseph Mallord William turner, *Landscape with a River and a Bay in the Background*. Courtesy of Wikimedia Commons (https://commons.wikimedia.org/wiki/File:Joseph_Mallord_William_Turner_-_Landscape_with_a_River_and_a_Bay_in_the_Background_-_WGA23174.jpg)
P10	Yonah Freemark (Yale College, '06)
P12	Shuchen Dong
P12	Robin Hengyuan Yang
P15	Shiqi Li
P88 bottom right	Raoul-Auger Feuillet, *Choregraphie*, 1701 The book is in the public domain (https://publicdomainreview.org/collection/choregraphie-1701)
P22, 23, 62, 63, 102, 103	Ruike Liu
P98, 100, 101	Rhea Schmid
P121	Rhea Schmid

Images in each student section are their own.